SANTA ANA PUBLIC LIBRARY
D0609294

QUETZALS
and Other Latin American Birds
QUETZALES
y otras aves de Latinoamérica

Zella Williams
Traducción al español: Ma. Pilar Obregón

PowerKiDS press. & Editorial Buenas Letras™
New York

Published in 2010 by The Rosen Publishing Group, Inc.
29 East 21st Street, New York, NY 10010

First Edition

Editor: Joanne Randolph
Book Design: Kate Laczynski
Photo Researcher: Jessica Gerweck

Photo Credits: Cover, p. 1 Kevin Schafer/Getty Images; pp. 5, 15 Roy Toft/Getty Images; p. 7 R H Productions/Getty Images; p. 9 © Sergio Dorantes/Corbis; p. 11 © Galen Rowell/Corbis; p. 13 © Michael & Patricia Fogden/Corbis; p. 17 © Natalie Fobes/Corbis; p. 19 Stuart Westmorland/Getty Images; p. 21 Joel Sartore/Getty Images.

Library of Congress Cataloging-in-Publication Data

Williams, Zella.
Quetzals and other Latin American birds = Quetzales y otras aves de Latinoamérica / Zella Williams. — 1st ed.
p. cm. — (Animals of Latin America = Animales de Latinoamérica)
Includes index.
ISBN 978-1-4042-8126-4 (library binding) — ISBN 978-1-4358-3380-7 (pbk.) — ISBN 978-1-4358-3381-4 (6-pack)
1. Quetzals—Latin America—Juvenile literature. 2. Birds—Latin America—Juvenile literature. I. Title. II. Title: Quetzales y otras aves de Latinoamérica.
QL696.T7W55 2010
598.7'3—dc22

2009002971

Manufactured in the United States of America

Contents

The Snake-Bird.........4
Symbol of Freedom.........8
Quetzal Home and Life.........12
Toucans and Macaws.........18
Birds in Danger.........22
Glossary.........23
Index and Web Sites.........24

Contenido

El ave-serpiente.........4
Símbolo de libertad.........8
La vida y el hogar del quetzal.........12
Tucanes y guacamayos.........18
Aves en peligro.........22
Glosario.........23
Índice y páginas de Internet.........24

There are thousands of colorful birds in the rain forests of Latin America. The quetzal has been considered to be one of the most beautiful of these birds since **ancient** times. The first people to live in **Mesoamerica** called this bird a snake-bird. This name came from its long tail feathers. These feathers look like shiny green snakes.

Miles de aves multicolores vuelan en las selvas tropicales de Latinoamérica. Desde tiempos **antiguos**, el quetzal ha sido considerado una de las más bellas de estas aves. Los indígenas de **Mesoamérica** llamaban al quetzal “ave-serpiente”. Esto se debe a las largas plumas de la cola del quetzal. Estas plumas parecen serpientes verdes.

Ancient Mesoamericans thought that quetzals connected the sky and the earth.

Los indígenas de Mesoamérica creían que el quetzal conectaba el cielo con la tierra.

The quetzal was **sacred** to the **Mayan people**. The Mayans caught the bird to take its feathers. However, if a person killed a quetzal, that person was put to death. The **Aztecs** and other Mesoamericans believed in a creator god, called Quetzalcoatl, the feathered snake. The quetzal was a **symbol** of this god.

El quetzal era un ave **sagrada** para los **mayas**. Los mayas lo capturaban y usaban sus alas. Sin embargo, si alguien mataba a un quetzal, esa persona era condenada a muerte. Los **aztecas** y otros grupos indígenas de Mesoamérica creían en Quetzalcoatl, un dios al que llamaban serpiente emplumada. El quetzal era el **símbolo** de Quetzalcoatl.

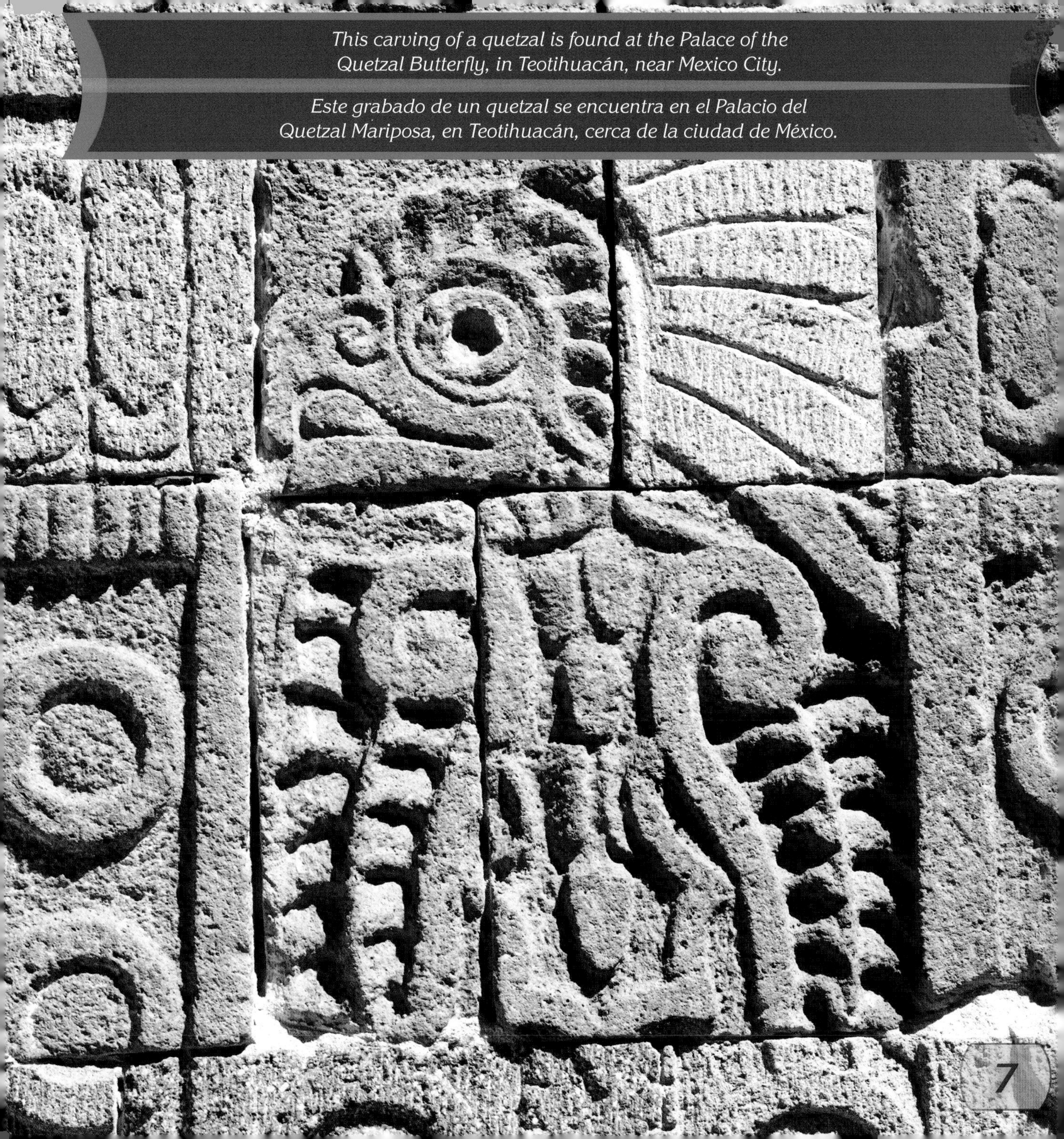

This carving of a quetzal is found at the Palace of the Quetzal Butterfly, in Teotihuacán, near Mexico City.

Este grabado de un quetzal se encuentra en el Palacio del Quetzal Mariposa, en Teotihuacán, cerca de la ciudad de México.

The importance of the quetzal has not faded since ancient times. Native people in Latin America still make beautiful masks, clothing, and other things using colorful quetzal feathers. Today the bird is the official symbol of Guatemala. Its picture can be seen on Guatemala's flag. The bird stands for freedom.

La importancia del quetzal no se ha perdido con el paso del tiempo. Los indígenas de Latinoamérica aún hacen máscaras y prendas con las plumas del quetzal. Actualmente, el quetzal es el ave oficial de Guatemala. La bandera de Guatemala tiene un quetzal en el centro. El quetzal en la bandera representa la Libertad.

This Mexican child is dressed for the Quetzal Dance, which dates back to ancient times. The headdress is meant to be like the quetzal's colorful feathers.

Este chico está vestido para la Danza del Quetzal. Esta danza se ha realizado en México durante cientos de años. El penacho representa las plumas multicolores del quetzal.

Guatemalan money is called the quetzal, too. This comes from the fact that, long ago, people used to trade valuable goods for prized quetzal feathers. These feathers were valued as much as gold. Throughout Mesoamerica, only rulers and paintings or statues of the gods could wear quetzal feathers.

La moneda de Guatemala se llama quetzal. Esto se debe a que hace muchos años, las personas cambiaban objetos por las valiosas plumas del quetzal. Estas plumas valían tanto como el oro. En la antigua Mesoamérica, sólo los gobernadores y los dioses podían usar las plumas del quetzal.

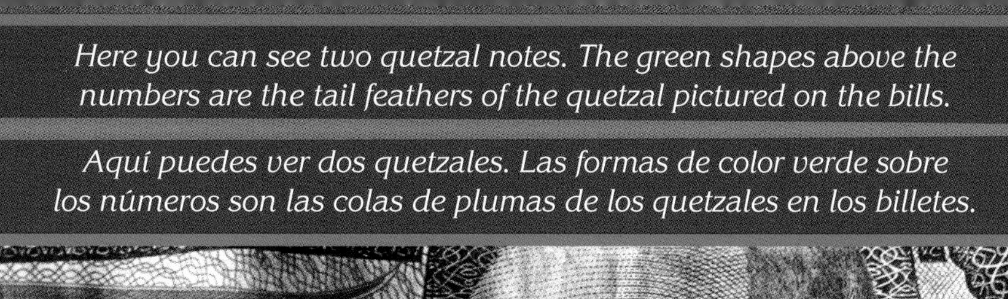

Here you can see two quetzal notes. The green shapes above the numbers are the tail feathers of the quetzal pictured on the bills.

Aquí puedes ver dos quetzales. Las formas de color verde sobre los números son las colas de plumas de los quetzales en los billetes.

You might wonder where this snake-bird lives. The quetzal can be found mainly in cloud forests from southern Mexico through Panama. Cloud forests are rain forests set high up in the mountains. There, quetzals make their nests inside dead trees. Full-grown quetzals eat mostly avocados, though they eat other fruit, too.

El quetzal vive en las selvas montañosas de Latinoamérica, desde el sur de México hasta Panamá. Una selva montañosa es una selva tropical que se encuentra en las cimas de las montañas. En estas selvas, los quetzales construyen sus nidos en los troncos de árboles secos. Los quetzales adultos comen aguacates y otras frutas.

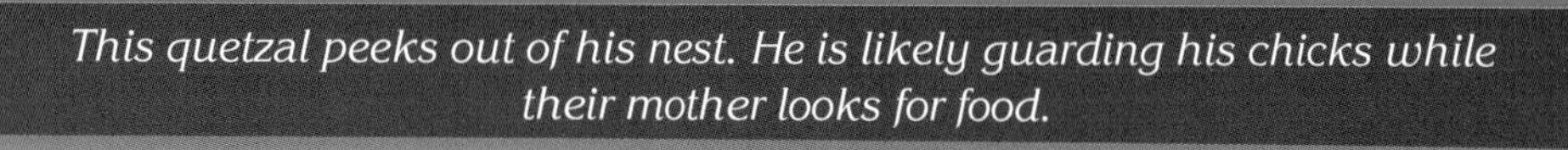

This quetzal peeks out of his nest. He is likely guarding his chicks while their mother looks for food.

Este quetzal se asoma en su nido. Es probable que esté cuidando a sus crías mientras mamá quetzal busca la comida.

The quetzal has shiny green feathers on its head, back, and wings. Its stomach is bright red. The tail has white, green, and blue feathers. The male quetzal has the long, snakelike feathers that have made the bird so well known. These long feathers can grow to be up to 3 feet (1 m) long.

El quetzal tiene plumas verdes y brillantes en la cabeza, el lomo y las alas. Las plumas del estómago son rojo brillante. La cola tiene plumas de color blanco, verde y azul. El quetzal macho tiene largas plumas en la cola, parecidas a una serpiente. Estas plumas, que han hecho tan famosos a los quetzales, pueden crecer hasta 3 pies (1 m) de largo.

The long tail feathers on the male quetzal, shown here, are called coverts. Females do not have these long feathers.

Las largas plumas de la cola del quetzal macho, que vemos aquí, se llaman cobertoras. Las hembras no tienen estas largas plumas.

When it is time to **mate**, the male quetzal flies in loops up into the sky and then dives back down. This show helps him find a female with whom he will mate. After the two birds mate, the female lays two light blue eggs in a nest that the male builds. He and the mother take turns sitting on the eggs and caring for the babies until they can live on their own.

Cuando es temporada de **apareamiento**, el quetzal macho vuela en círculos en el cielo antes de lanzarse hacia abajo. Esto le ayuda a encontrar a una hembra. Tras aparearse, la hembra pone dos huevos de color azul claro en un nido que ha sido construído por el macho. Tanto el macho como la hembra toman turnos sentándose sobre los huevos y cuidando de los bebés hasta que han crecido y pueden cuidarse por sí mismos.

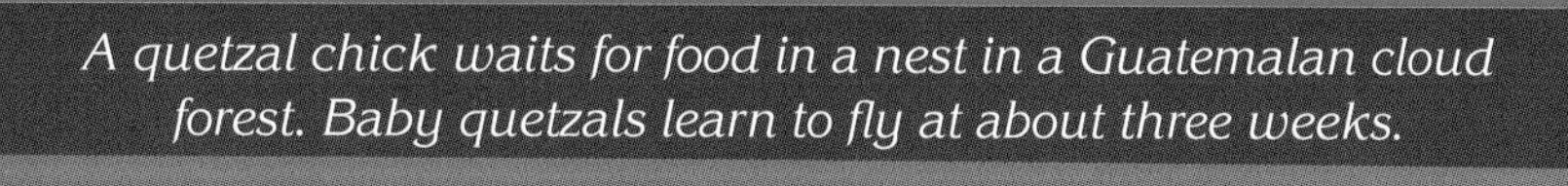

A quetzal chick waits for food in a nest in a Guatemalan cloud forest. Baby quetzals learn to fly at about three weeks.

Un polluelo de quetzal espera a ser alimentado en su nido, en un bosque montañoso de Guatemala. Los bebés de quetzal aprenden a volar a las tres semanas de nacidos.

The quetzal shares its rain forest home with another colorful bird. The toucan is known for its extra long, colorful bill. It, too, nests in tree holes and shares the care of its young with its mate. Ancient people in Latin America also considered the toucan sacred. They believed the bird connected the worlds of the living and the dead.

El quetzal comparte los cielos de la selva tropical con otra ave multicolor. El tucán es conocido por su largo pico. Como el quetzal, el tucán hace su nido en hoyos de los árboles y cuida de sus crías con su pareja. Los antiguos habitantes de Latinoamérica también consideraban sagrado al tucán. En su opinión, el tucán conectaba el mundo de los vivos con el de los muertos.

This keel-billed toucan is about 20 inches (51 cm) tall. It lives in rain forests from southern Mexico to northern Colombia and northeastern Venezuela.

Este tucán de gran pico mide cerca de 20 pulgadas (51 cm) de alto. Los tucanes viven en las selvas tropicales, desde el sur de México hasta el norte de Colombia y Venezuela.

Macaws live in rain forests and other places throughout Latin America. Colorful macaws are part of the parrot family. They eat fruit, nuts, and snails. Like the quetzal, many ancient people prized the feathers of these birds. They also felt that macaws carried messages between the living and the dead.

Los guacamayos viven en las selvas tropicales y otros lugares en Latinoamérica. Los coloridos guacamayos pertenecen a la familia de los loros. Los guacamayos comen frutas, frutos secos y caracoles. Como las del quetzal, las plumas de los guacamayos eran muy apreciadas. En la antigua Mesoamérica se creía que los guacamayos llevaban mensajes entre los vivos y los muertos.

Today the Bororo people of Brazil prize macaws. Red-and-green macaws, such as these, and scarlet macaws are the most important to the Bororo.

Actualmente, para los bororos de Brasil los guacamayos son muy apreciados. Para los bororos los guacamayos de plumas rojas y verdes, y los de color escarlata, son los más importantes.

Latin America is home to some of the world's most beautiful birds. It also has more kinds of birds than any other place in the world. Sadly, many of Latin America's birds, such as the quetzal, are in danger. We must find a way to keep the birds and their homes safe so they do not die out. How can you help?

Latinoamérica es el hogar de algunas de las aves más bellas del mundo. Pero además es el lugar con mayor variedad en el planeta. Desafortunadamente, muchas de las aves de Latinoamérica, como el quetzal, están en peligro.
Es importante que encontremos una manera de proteger a estas aves y sus hogares para que no desaparezcan.
Tú puedes ayudar. ¿Tienes alguna idea de cómo hacerlo?

Glossary

ancient (AYN-shent) Very old, from a long time ago.
Aztecs (AZ-teks) Native Americans of central Mexico.
mate (MAYT) To join together to make babies.
Mayan people (MY-en PEE-pul) Native Americans of southern Mexico and Central America.
Mesoamerica (MEH-zo-uh-mer-ih-kuh) Mexico and Central America.
sacred (SAY-kred) Highly respected and considered very important.
symbol (SIM-bul) An object or a picture that stands for something else.

Glosario

antiguos (los) Que son viejos, que tienen mucho tiempo.
apareamiento Juntarse para tener crías.
aztecas (los) Indígenas originarios del centro de México.
mayas (los) Indígenas originarios del sur de México y Centroamérica.
Mesoamérica Región de México y Centroamérica.
sagrado Muy respetado. Considerado muy importante.
símbolo (el) Un objeto o imagen que representa a otra cosa.

Index

A
Aztecs, 6

C
cloud forest, 12

F
feathers, 4, 6, 8, 10, 14, 20

G
god(s), 6, 10

M
macaw, 20
Mayan people, 6
Mesoamerica, 4, 10

P
picture, 8

Q
Quetzalcoatl, 6

R
rain forests, 4, 12, 20
rulers, 10

S
snake-bird, 4, 12
snake(s), 4, 6
symbol, 6, 8

T
toucan, 18

Índice

A
ave-serpiente, 4, 12
aztecas, 6

D
dios(es), 6, 10

G
gobernadores, 10
guacamayos, 20

M
mayas, 6
Mesoamérica, 4, 10

P
plumas, 4, 6, 8, 10, 14, 20

Q
Quetzalcoatl, 6

S
selva montañosa, 12
selvas tropicales, 4, 12, 20
serpiente(s), 4, 6
símbolo, 6, 8

T
tucán, 18

Web Sites / Páginas de Internet

Due to the changing nature of Internet links, PowerKids Press and Editorial Buenas Letras have developed an online list of Web sites related to the subject of this book. This site is updated regularly. Please use this link to access the list:
www.powerkidslinks.com/anla/quetzal/

D0609293

A Painful History of Crime

Prisons and Prisoners

John Townsend

Chicago, Illinois

For information, address the publisher:
Raintree, 100 N. La Salle, Suite 1200
Chicago, IL 60602
Customer Service: 888-363-4266
Visit our website at www.raintreelibrary.com

Printed and bound in China by South China Printing Company

10 09 08 07 06
10 9 8 7 6 5 4 3 2 1

Library of Congress Cataloging-in-Publication Data

Townsend, John, 1955-
Prisons and prisoners / John Townsend.
p. cm. -- (A painful history of crime)
Includes bibliographical references and index.
ISBN 1-4109-2053-4 (library binding - hardcover) -- ISBN 1-4109-2058-5 (pbk.)
1. Prisons--Juvenile literature. 2. Prisoners--Juvenile literature. I. Title.
HV8705.T68 2005
365--dc22
2005012516

Acknowledgments
The author and publisher are grateful to the following for permission to reproduce copyright material: Acestock **8–9** (focus estonia); Alamy Images pp. **1**, **8**, **36–37**; **14** (William Owens), **9** (Bildarchiv Monheim GmbH), **6–7** (culliganphoto), **38** (Photofusion); Corbis pp. **21** (Royalty Free), **16–17** (Historical Picture Archive), **43** (Anton Daix), **4**, **7**, **32**, **36** (Bettmann), **5t**, **11** (Charles & Josette Lenars), **1(** (Charles E. Rotkin), **4–5**, **22–23** (Gianni Dagli Orti), **6** (Jan Brecelj), **26–27** (Lake County Museum), **28** (Minnesota Historical Society), **30–31**, **35** (Reuters), **42–43** (Shannon Stapleton/Reuters), **42** (Tim Wright); Getty Images pp. **10** (Photodisc), **33** (AFP), **5m**, **5b**,**18–19**, **23**, **24–25**, **29**, **30**, **37** (Hulton Archive), **13**, **20–21** (Time & Life Pictures); Mary Evans Picture Library pp. **12**, **15**, **22**, **24**; Oz Images **19**; Photographers Direct **12–13** (John Blythe); Rex Features **38–39**; The Kobal Collection **34** (Corona/Allied Artists); Topfoto pp. **41** (Bob Daemmrich / The Image Works); **40–41** (Sean Cayton/The Image Works); Unknown **27**.

Cover photograph of chain gang reproduced with permission of Getty Images/Time & Life Pictures.

Every effort has been made to contact copyright holders of any material reproduced in this book. Any omissions will be rectified in subsequent printings if notice is given to the publisher.

Contents

Lock Them Up....................4

Prisons Long Ago....................6

Tough Times for Prisoners....................12

Time for Change....................20

Prisoners of War....................28

Leaving the Past Behind....................34

New Ways....................38

Prisons in the News....................42

Find Out More....................44

Glossary....................46

Index....................48

Any words appearing in the text in bold, **like this,** are explained in the glossary. You can also look out for them in the "Word Bank" at the bottom of each page.

Lock Them Up

The rattle of chains and the clang of iron doors echoed through the night. It was hard to sleep on the cold stone floor. The rats did not help. Nor did the groans from the prisoners hung up on hooks on the moldy prison walls. Stale bread and dirty water were pushed through the bars once a day. There was not even a bucket for a toilet. Many prisoners could be locked together in a tiny, smelly cell for years . . .

Is this what prisons were really like hundreds of years ago? In fact, many were far worse. Are any still like this today?

Prisoners are set free from the Bastille prison in Paris, France, in 1789.

Behind bars

"Lock them up and throw away the key!" For hundreds of years this was people's idea of what to do with criminals. Some people still say it today! But prisons and what we think about prisoners have changed a lot over time.

Word Bank deter put off or stop

What are prisons for?

The first prisons were built thousands of years ago. Since then, billions of people have been locked up. Prisons today still do some of the jobs they did long ago:

- keep **suspects** safe and **secure** until their case is heard in court.
- pay back criminals for committing crimes. Their freedom is taken away as a punishment.
- keep dangerous criminals out of the way. Prisons protect us by keeping criminals off the streets.
- **deter** people from offending again or from doing wrong in the first place. If people think they will get sent to prison for committing a crime, they might obey the law.

Find out later . . .

How were prisoners tortured in the past?

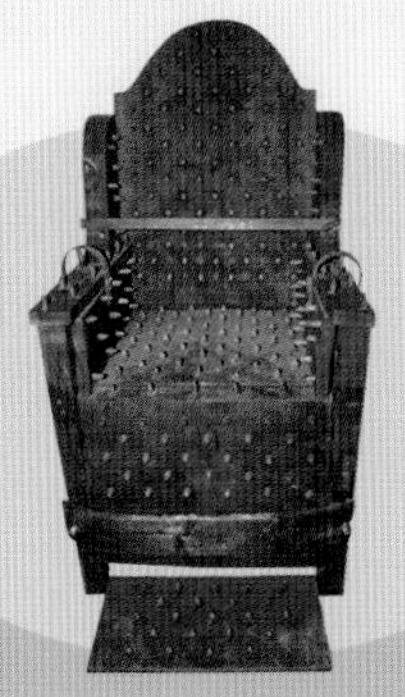

When were prisoners chained up in ships and sent across the world?

Who worked hard to take the pain out of prisons?

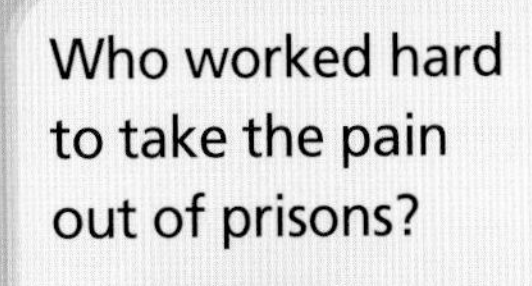

secure keep safe or locked up
suspect someone thought to have done wrong

Prisons Long Ago

In ancient times prisons were used differently from the way we use them today. More than 2,500 years ago, the Romans imprisoned people who were waiting to go to **trial** or to be **executed.** Criminals were not given prison **sentences** for a set number of years like they are today. Prison was just a "holding space" before the real punishment began.

You can visit one of the old Roman prisons today. It is under Capitoline Hill in Rome, Italy. This dark, damp underground **dungeon** once held prisoners waiting to be **crucified.** For serious crimes, prisoners could be left there to starve to death.

Egypt

We know from written records that there were prisons in Egypt more than 4,000 years ago. But we do not know much about them or what they were like. Criminals were probably locked inside until they were put to death.

Ancient writings found in Egypt tell us about their prisons.

Word Bank

crucified put to death by nailing the hands and feet to a cross

Past secrets

Many other old prisons are now museums. Langzisha prison in Tibet was opened to visitors in 2005. Although it is almost 400 years old, it has been **restored** for tourists to visit. While the building was being restored, some of the prison's grisly secrets were uncovered. The tools used to punish prisoners were found. Some tools were for digging out the prisoners' eyes. Others were for cutting off ears, hands, and feet. Perhaps worst of all were the blades used for skinning people alive. This prison must have been a truly terrible place.

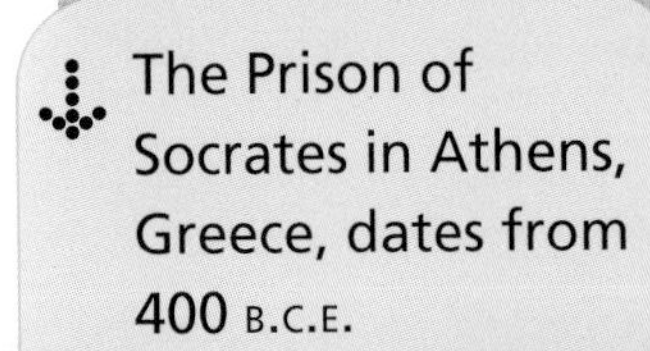

The Prison of Socrates in Athens, Greece, dates from 400 B.C.E.

Roman prisoners had to fight wild animals in the Colosseum in Rome to entertain spectators.

Greece

The Greeks had prisons 2,000 years ago. Most criminals had to pay a **fine**, but if they did not have enough money, they went to prison instead. The law did not set down fixed prison sentences the way it does today.

restored rebuilt and made as it once was
sentence punishment set by a court of law

The dungeon

The word *dungeon* comes from the French word *donjon*. A castle's *donjon* was the great tower. This was sometimes used as a prison tower and became called a dungeon. Today the word *dungeon* means "a dark underground cell."

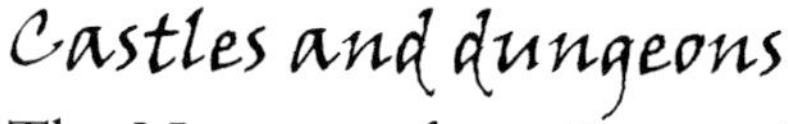

Castles and dungeons

The Normans from France invaded England in 1066 and built many castles. These strong buildings were to keep important people and soldiers safe. In time, they also had places inside for locking people away. It depended who the prisoners were as to how well they were treated. Rich people would probably be taken care of, but a **peasant** or a soldier would have a hard time in prison.

Some castles across Europe and the Middle East had very small dungeons. These were called **oubliettes.** This word comes from the French word *oublier*, which means "to forget." Prisoners thrown into oubliettes were soon forgotten about and left to die.

A black hole

The only way into the pitch black oubliette was through a trap door in its ceiling. The prisoner was sometimes tied to a rope and lowered into the stinking hole. Other times, the prisoner was simply thrown in. The oubliette was often just a pit about three feet (one meter) across and ten feet (three meters) deep. Sometimes the pit filled with cold, muddy water seeping up through the bottom.

Dungeons were dark, cold, damp, and miserable.

The Black Tower in Turkey has an oubliette at the end of a long, dark passage. Prisoners were forced along the passage before they fell down into it. Some would probably never see the light of day again.

Word Bank

oubliette dungeon with an opening only at the top, found in some old castles

Castle prisons

Lincoln Castle was one of the many Norman castles built in England. From 1068 prisoners were held there. In fact, prisoners were kept there on and off over the next 800 years.

Much of Dover Castle, built by the Normans, is still standing today.

A prisoner in an oubliette would have one last glimpse of daylight before the trapdoor closed shut.

peasant poor person or farmworker

The Tower of London

When the Norman leader William the Conqueror took over England, he needed a strong and **secure** building to keep him safe. In 1070 he began building the Tower of London. It soon became used as a prison, too. You can visit it today and see where many prisoners were put to death.

More prisons, more pain

The years from 800 to 1500 are now called the Middle Ages. In Europe at this time prisons began to be built for "ordinary" criminals. About 900 years ago, the Tower of London (below) became a prison and a place of punishment.

The Tower was not just the place where royal prisoners had their heads chopped off. It was where ordinary prisoners were punished. One prison cell was just the size of a person bent over. It was called "the little ease." A prisoner put inside was so cramped that he or she was unable to lie down or stand up.

Word Bank

bishop leader in the Church of England
pope leader of the Roman Catholic Church

Party time

Prison was not always a painful experience. Sometimes it could almost be pleasant, even in the Tower of London. This was the case for some rich prisoners. The first prisoner here was the **bishop** of Durham. He was sent to the Tower in 1100 on the orders of King Henry I, for charging people too much **tax**.

In prison, the bishop was allowed visitors from outside to join him for big feasts. During one of these feasts, he made his guards drunk. Then he managed to escape. Using a rope smuggled to him in a wine barrel, he climbed out through one of the Tower's windows. He escaped to France.

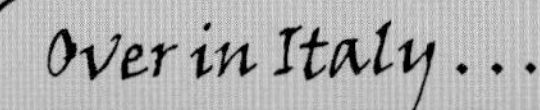

Over in Italy . . .

In Rome in 1298, the **pope** said that criminals could be sent to prison for a set period of time, or for life. This began more organized **sentencing** for different crimes. At the same time, towns began building more prisons for **common people**.

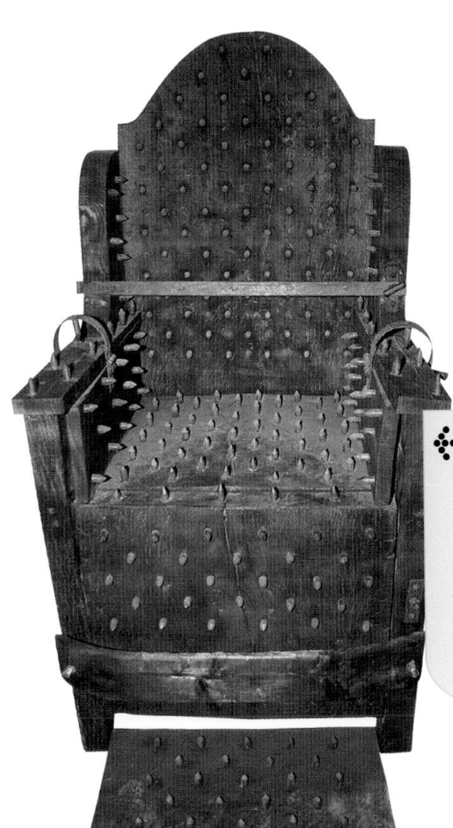

As if prison was not bad enough, instruments of **torture** such as this chair of spikes were used in the Middle Ages.

tax charge set by leaders or government to pay for public services
torture causing someone great pain

Tough Times for Prisoners

Did you know?

By the 1590s many people in England were put in prisons—just for being poor. But they still needed money even there. Prisoners had to pay jailers for food and blankets. Without any money at all, a prisoner would be treated very badly.

The 1500s to 1700s were times of great change across the world. Sailors from Europe began to explore the world. They brought back goods from new lands and many **traders** grew rich. But the richer people grew, the more they became targets for thieves. Crime began to increase.

The poor

In the United Kingdom, the richer some people became, the more they hated the poor who begged in the streets. Begging began to be seen as a crime. Beggars would be beaten, and could be dragged off to prison. Many were not seen again. Prison life was very cruel. It was also full of rats and disease.

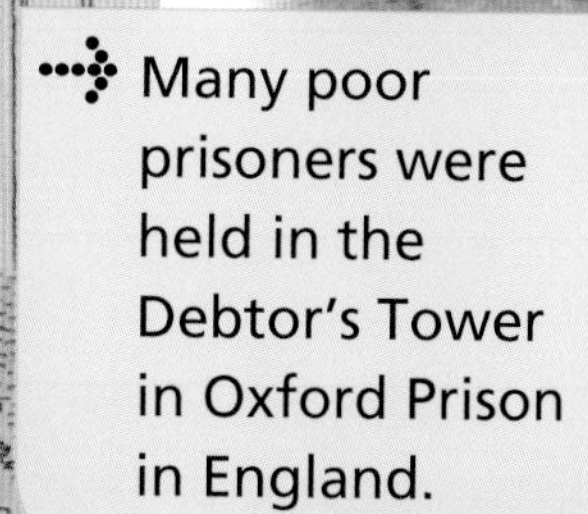

Many poor prisoners were held in the Debtor's Tower in Oxford Prison in England.

Word Bank **poverty** having no money or possessions

Prisons arrive in America

At the start of the 1600s, Europeans saw how to escape from the crime and **poverty** around them. They could start a new life in the "new world." Many people sailed to America . . . taking crime with them. Prisons were soon needed in the new world, too.

1625: Fort Amsterdam was a Dutch fort that was built in what is now Manhattan in New York City. It had **dungeons** to hold prisoners such as rowdy soldiers or people who could not pay their bills.

1632: The Massachusetts Bay Colony built the first proper prison. It was a simple wooden building for locking up criminals. Soon there were many more prisons.

Europeans arrive in North America

1492: The first voyage of Christopher Columbus of Spain arrived at Cuba in the West Indies. He returned home to tell of a "new world." Other explorers soon followed.

1585: The first English settlers arrived in America at Roanoke Island, North Carolina.

1620: The "Pilgrim Fathers" of England arrived in Massachusetts in the ship *the Mayflower* (below).

trader person who buys and sells goods to make money

Prison homes

Many prisoners in the United Kingdom in the 1600s were **debtors.** A debtor was someone who owed other people money. If they could not pay their bills, they were locked away until they could. To get the money to pay their debts, people had to work hard in prison for a very low wage. They could also sell their food to other prisoners. Often, their whole family would have to live in the debtors' prison, too.

By 1650, London was building more **workhouses** where the poor went to work. These were not prisons where criminals were locked up, but they had very strict rules. People who lived in them had to work very hard, just like in prisons.

Helping the very poor

The name for a person with no home or money was a **pauper.** Although many paupers were seen as criminals, some English towns tried to help. They provided food and a room for the night . . . but the pauper would have to work for it. In the 1600s, anyone pretending to be a pauper to get a free meal would be beaten.

This building in Suffolk, England, was built as a workhouse for the poor.

Word Bank

pauper very poor person who had to beg or get help from a workhouse

When is a prison not a prison?

An English law in 1697 made all **paupers** wear badges. Without a badge, no one would get work or food at a workhouse. Arriving at a workhouse, paupers were stripped, washed, and made to wear a uniform. Their own clothes were locked away until they could afford to leave.

Husbands and wives were not allowed to talk to each other. If they did, they could be beaten.

> *Any pauper in this workhouse shall be punished if he/she:*
>
> - *makes any noise when silence is ordered to be kept*
> - *refuses to work*
> - *climbs over any fence or wall surrounding the workhouse.*

However, many paupers could not read these rules!

Houses of correction

In the late 1600s London began to build more workhouses called "houses of correction." These workhouses were to stop people from begging. Paupers were sent to work. One of the jobs they had to do was break up rocks into small pieces. It was hard work. All the broken stones were sold to make roads.

This is an illustration of women and children in a prison yard in London.

workhouse large house where the poor stayed and worked

Prison ships

Where could prisoners be put so they could never escape? An answer in the 1700s was "out to sea." Old ships floating off the coast were filled with prisoners. Life on board was grim—even worse in stormy seas.

Great Britain and America used prison ships when they fought each other in 1775. When enemy soldiers were caught, they had to be kept out of the way. So they were put in ships and treated like criminals. Prisoners of war had a hard time. The British kept prison ships in New York Harbor. About 11,000 American soldiers died in these ships—more than in all the battles. That is how bad they were.

American war

Great Britain ruled America through the 1700s. But by 1770 many Americans wanted to rule their own country. From 1775 to 1783 the British fought Americans over this. Many enemy soldiers were captured by each side and kept as prisoners. The Americans won the war and became an **independent** country in 1783.

A celebration of the 200th anniversary of the Revolutionary War in New York Harbor in 1976.

Word Bank **death sentence** being sent to prison before being put to death

Death on water

Being sent to a floating prison was like a **death sentence.** The stinking ships were full of filth, rats, and disease. Over a thousand prisoners could be packed into one creaking ship. American prisoners in New York Harbor died from illness and bad food. When their British guards opened the hatches each morning, they shouted to the prisoners below, "Bring out your dead."

> When a man died he was carried up on deck and laid there until the next morning. Bodies were carried on shore in heaps and taken in carts to a big hole, to be thrown in together.
>
> *(Christopher Vail, American prisoner, 1781. Prison ship HMS Jersey)*

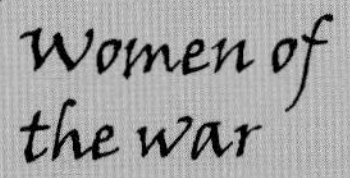

Women of the war

Thousands of women worked for the American and British armies during the Revolutionary War. Many were the wives of soldiers. A lot of them were taken prisoner, too. After a battle near New York in 1779, 52 British women became prisoners of the American Army. They were taken to prison camps on land rather than to prison ships.

This painting shows British prison ships in about 1800.

independent free from outside control or support

Shipped to Australia

Britain had a growing problem in the 1700s. There were too many prisoners. In the past, many of these criminals would have been hung. But people were now thinking it was better to send criminals to prison instead. So prisons soon filled up. What could be done? The answer was simple. Put prisoners on ships, send them across the world, and leave them there. That would get rid of the problem!

Australia was part of the British **Empire** and seemed the perfect place to send thousands of criminals. Anyone found **guilty** of minor crimes such as stealing bread could be sent away, never to return. This was called **transportation.**

Sent away

About 160,000 British prisoners were sent to Australia between the 1780s and 1860s. Of these prisoners, 25,000 were women. Some of them were guilty of no more than stealing a scrap of cloth to make clothes for their family.

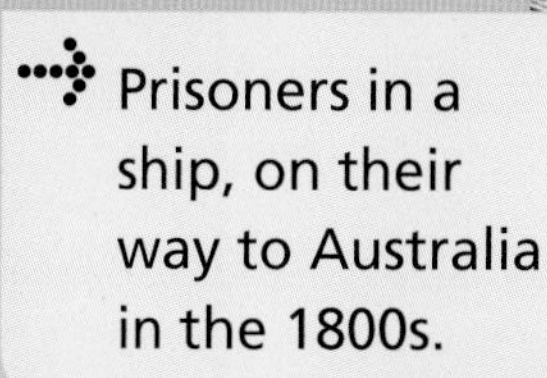

Prisoners in a ship, on their way to Australia in the 1800s.

Word Bank **empire** area ruled by one country

Pain and misery

During a terrible sea journey lasting six months or more, prisoners often died from illness, hunger, or from being beaten. As soon as they arrived in Australia, they were started working, for example carrying timber and rocks. Some prisoners were chained together and the chains often cut into their bodies.

Any prisoner upsetting a guard would be beaten and thrown in a prison cell. Some of these small cells were totally dark, with thick walls. Prisoners were fed salted meat and water, with nothing else. Many became ill from such a poor diet. They longed to see home again, but very few ever did.

Prison museum

Maitland Gaol (above) in New South Wales, Australia, is now open to the public as a museum. In 1848 the prison saw its last public hanging and its first prisoners from Newcastle, England. The prison was in use until January 1998 as one of the toughest in Australia.

transportation shipping of criminals across the world to prisons or hard labor

Time for Change

Paying the price

In the 1700s prisons were so dirty that many prisoners died of diseases they caught inside. Many of them were not even **guilty** of crimes other than being poor. As prisoners had to pay to be let out of prison, they did not stand a chance of being set free. A law stopped this "**discharge** fee" in 1774.

By the end of the 1700s, many people in Great Britain and America were worried about the cruel way prisoners were being treated. But it was well into the 1800s before real changes to prisons started.

New ideas

In 1777, a **high sheriff** named John Howard visited all the prisons in England and wrote a report of his visits. He was shocked by the way prisons were run. He said prisoners needed more space and better food. Guards should be paid by the government rather than by the prisoners. He even said prisons should help prisoners rather than just punish them. No one could imagine such an idea.

Prisoners were allowed to exercise in the prison yard at Fleet Prison in London.

Word Bank

high sheriff officer of the government in charge of enforcing the law

Pain behind bars

John Howard and others did a lot to change prisons for the better. Even so, it took many more years for prisons to change. This report was from another **politician** named Thomas Buxton in 1818:

> "The moment a prisoner enters prison, irons are hammered on to him. At night he is locked up in a narrow cell with the worst of thieves. **Vagrants'** rags are alive and moving with fleas. The prisoner may have to share a bed with someone with a foul disease. He may spend his days with no fresh air and exercise . . . being half starved."

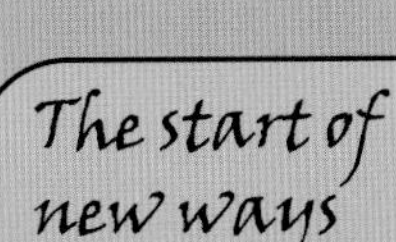

The start of new ways

After John Howar report, prisons in the 1800s were built with larger cells. Prisoners we given clean uniforms. They were no longer ke in chains. Male an female prisoners were no longer kept together.

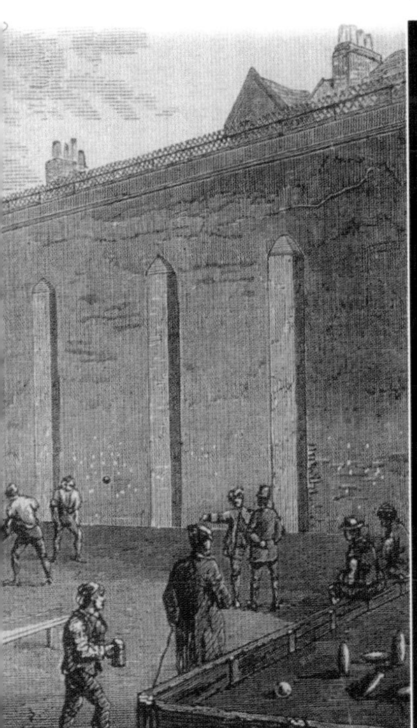

politician person who takes part in a political party or in government
vagrant person with no job, money, or home who wanders from place to place

The Bastille

To many people in Paris, The Bastille was a **symbol** of the cruel power of rich rulers in the 1700s. This prison was hated because of the stories of horrible **torture**. Its walls were very thick and its towers were 98 feet (30 meters) high. No prisoner was ever likely to escape—until a mob had other ideas . . .

Big changes

The Bastille was an ancient fort in Paris, France. It became a terrible prison, especially for anyone who upset the French kings and queens. In 1789 many French people decided to get rid of this prison once and for all. On July 14, they attacked it. In fact, the jail only had seven prisoners inside at the time. Even so, they were guarded by soldiers with cannons. But that did not stop 1,000 angry people from storming the prison. In the attack, 98 of them were killed as they set the prisoners free. Today, July 14 is known as Bastille Day in France.

This was how many prisoners at the Bastille were kept chained.

Word Bank **civilized** behaving with high standards and respect for others

Walnut Street

The first prisons built in the United States were just like those in the UK. Men and women were locked into one crowded area, with straw on the floor to sleep on. The smell was terrible. Fights were common.

Walnut Street Jail in Philadelphia.

In 1791 the Walnut Street Goal (Jail) opened in Philadelphia. It was different. Called the "first **penitentiary** in the world," it used new ideas. Treating prisoners in a **civilized** way was thought to make them more civilized themselves. People who ran the prison believed they could actually change criminals for the better. They gave prisoners clean, private cells. Walnut Street Goal was a big step toward change in prisons across the United States.

The painting shows the storming of the Bastille in July 1789.

New ways

Walnut Street Goal became known as the Pennsylvania System of running prisons. It used times of silence to help prisoners think and study. For the first time, prisoners were helped to change rather than "left to suffer." This system began to be used in other prisons in the 1800s.

penitentiary type of prison
symbol something that stands for, or represents, something else

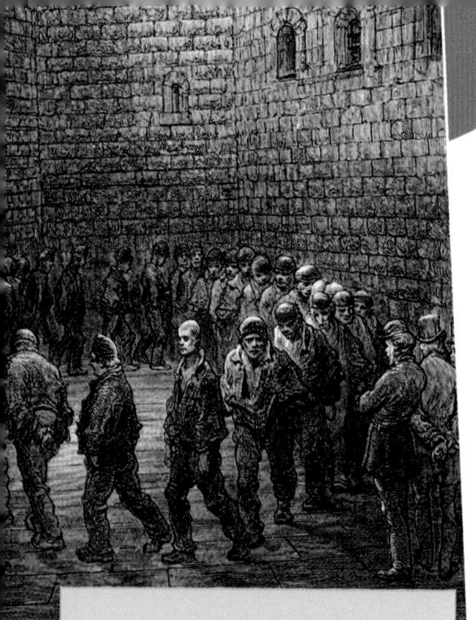

Prisoners at Newgate were not allowed to speak when exercising in the yard.

Newgate Prison

Newgate Prison in London was known for being tough. It only began to change for the better in the 1800s. Even so, like many prisons in the United Kingdom, Newgate had the Law of Silence until 1898. This law meant prisoners were not allowed to speak when out of their cells for meals, work, or exercise.

Some of the "work" at Newgate was not very pleasant:

The work on the tread wheel was to walk up the wheel. You did 10 minutes on and 5 minutes off, for 8 hours. Other work was picking out threads from old ropes. These were sold for making string or stuffing mattresses. It was "money for old rope."

Old and new

The first prison at Newgate in London was built in 1188. It was rebuilt in 1782 after prisoners damaged it in **riots**. Every Monday morning until 1868, large crowds gathered there to watch prisoners be **hung**. A good seat at one of the windows overlooking the **gallows** was expensive, but people were happy to pay to see prisoners killed.

Word Bank

gallows wooden structure from which prisoners were hung

Elizabeth Fry

It took a woman with new ideas to speed up the change that was needed in prisons such as Newgate. This woman was Elizabeth Fry. She heard how prisoners had to sleep on bare stone floors, and newborn babies of prisoners had no clothing. She began to make clothes for these babies and in 1813 went to see Newgate prison for herself.

"Nearly 300 women and children were all crowded together. They all slept on the floor. At times there were 120 in one ward without mats for bedding and many of them were nearly naked. Everything is filthy and the smell is quite disgusting."

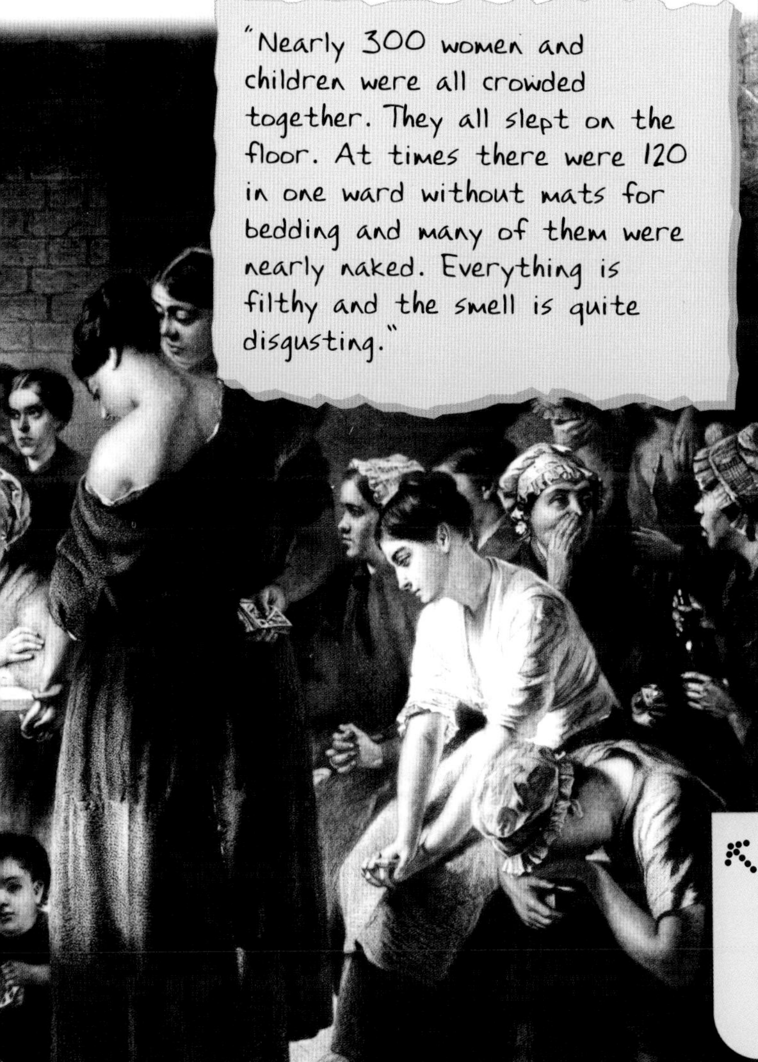

Elizabeth Fry visited women in Newgate Prison and read the bible to them.

Woman with a mission

Elizabeth Fry was born in England in 1780. In 1800 she married a rich London **merchant**. From 1813 until her death in 1845, she worked to improve life for prisoners. She traveled around Europe in her work to make prisons cleaner and more comfortable.

merchant buyer and seller of goods to make money
riot cause public violence and disorder

Same but different

The name of Newgate Prison was well known in New York for the first 30 years of the 1800s. But New York grew so fast at this time that Newgate could not cope with the number of prisoners. A new jail had to take over—the famous Sing Sing Prison.

Newgate, New York

Newgate was the name of New York's first state prison. It opened in 1797. When prisoners arrived there, they were stripped, washed, and given a prison uniform. By 1815, **first-termers** wore striped suits. Second-termers wore brown jackets and trousers. Third-termers had to feel shame and wear a blue cap with the number "3"on the front.

Each prisoner had to pay for his uniform. There was also a charge for travel to prison and 15 cents a day for food. The prison kept a record of each prisoner's work and earnings. On his release, each prisoner was paid. All the costs of his stay were **deducted.**

Word Bank **first-termer** prisoner who is in prison for the first time

Leading the way

Meals in Newgate were always eaten in silence. All swearing, singing, and whistling were forbidden. Although these rules were strict, U.S. prisons had many new ideas. They even had classrooms and rooms set aside for worship. This idea was far ahead of prisons in Europe.

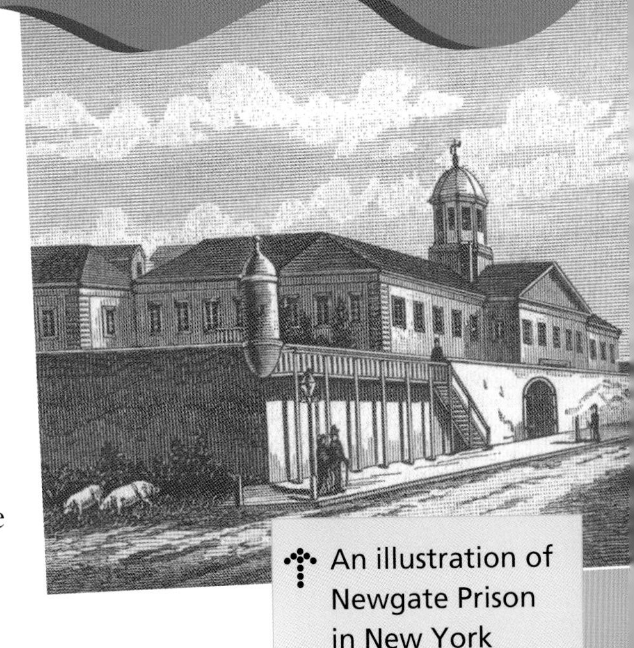

An illustration of Newgate Prison in New York from the 1800s.

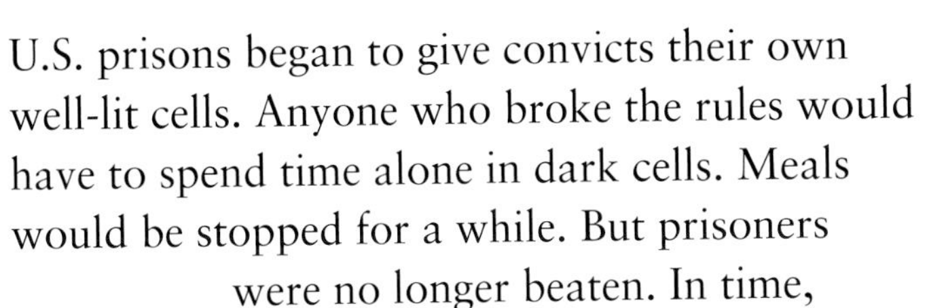

U.S. prisons began to give convicts their own well-lit cells. Anyone who broke the rules would have to spend time alone in dark cells. Meals would be stopped for a while. But prisoners were no longer beaten. In time, prisons in Europe began to follow these ideas. By the mid 1800s, change was on its way.

If prisoners managed to escape, they would soon be noticed in their prison uniforms.

Fire

In 1803, 40 prisoners got into Newgate's yard and started a fire. When twenty of them tried to escape over the walls, the guards shot and killed four of them. The following year, prisoners escaped after locking guards in a room and setting it on fire. One prisoner had second thoughts and opened the door, saving the guards' lives.

deducted taken away

Prisoners of War

In times of war, enemy soldiers are often caught and taken as prisoners. They are kept in prison camps until the war ends. Long ago it was different. The ancient Greeks would kill anyone they found from an enemy side. The rules of war today make it clear that prisoners of war are not criminals and must be treated fairly.

North and south

The Civil War lasted from 1861 to 1865. The North and the South fought because of their different views on how to run the country. In the end, the 23 Union states in the North beat the 11 Confederate states in the South. About 600,000 men were killed during the Civil War. Almost as many were taken prisoner.

The Civil War

Nearly four million soldiers fought in the **Civil War** from 1861 to 1865. More than 400,000 of them were taken prisoner at some stage. The problem was where to put them all. Prison camps became crowded and filthy.

A painting of the Battle of Nashville in 1862, during the Civil War.

Word Bank **civil war** when soldiers from the same country fight against each other

Punished

Up to 50,000 men died in prison camps from wounds, disease, or from drinking dirty water. Life as a prisoner of war could be grim. Most prison camps had special cells for those who broke the rules.

The "white oak" was a **dungeon**, 10 feet (3 meters) deep. This dark foul hole was entered by a trap door. I was thrown inside for trying to get a bucket of water at a hospital well. I spent the most wretched hours of my life in that terrible place. I could not see my hand in front of my face in such total darkness.

—Milton Asbury Ryan (1842–1916, Confederate soldier)

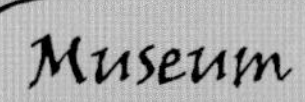

Museum

A prison camp was quickly built at Andersonville, Georgia. It was used for 14 months of the war. In that time more than 45,000 Union soldiers were kept there. But it could only cope with a fraction of that number. Almost 13,000 prisoners died inside. Today, the site is a prisoner of war museum.

Belle Island Confederate prison camp in Virginia, during the Civil War.

Getting home

When World War I ended in 1918, all the prisoners of war locked up in German prisons were free to leave. The prison guards just left their posts and went home. That meant many American and Australian prisoners had to find their way back home from the middle of Europe!

World War

In the last two World Wars, the Germans captured many soldiers, including thousands from the United Kingdom, Australia, and the United States. World War I was from 1914 to 1918. World War II was from 1939 to 1945.

> The Germans put us in a prison. They gave us hardly any food. We may have had a slice of bread a day, little else. We had to build **dugouts**, huts, or carry and load bombs. All that, on just one slice of bread in the morning and at midday a pot of soup. It was just like water.
>
> *(Horace Ganson, 16th Battalion, Australian Imperial Force, captured in World War I)*

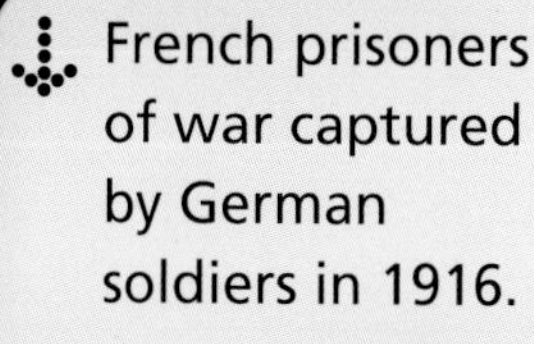

French prisoners of war captured by German soldiers in 1916.

Word Bank **dugout** shelter dug in a hillside or in the ground

World War II

Colditz Castle was a famous prison in Germany during World War II. It was built high up on a rock and heavily guarded. The Germans said it was "escape-proof." They were wrong. In just over five years, there were many escape attempts. About 120 prisoners managed to get out. Most of them were caught again.

By the time the United States freed Colditz from the Germans in 1945, more than 30 prisoners had escaped and reached home. Some of them had dug tunnels. Others climbed from high windows or dressed as guards and walked out through the gates. So much for the prison being escape-proof!

Not many people knew this . . .

In 1946, the year after the end of World War II, German prisoners of war were still held in the United Kingdom and the United States to work on farms. Up to one fifth of the farm work in the United Kingdom was being done by German prisoners of war.

This is Colditz Castle in Saxony, Germany.

The rules of war

A law makes countries care for their prisoners of war. In 1929, the Geneva Convention set down a law that protects prisoners—from the time of being captured to the time of release. It is **illegal** to torture a prisoner of war. He or she only has to give a name, date of birth, rank, and service number.

Captured

In the last 100 years, millions of people have been put in prison because of who they were, rather than for what they did. **Political prisoners** have been locked up because their country's leaders have seen them as a threat. Some cruel leaders have sent people to prison just because of their **race.**

Vietnam

In the 1960s the U.S. sent troops to Vietnam to stop the government in the north from taking over the south. They did not succeed. It was a difficult war that did not end until 1976. About 3.2 million Vietnamese were killed. About 58,000 Americans lost their lives. Hundreds were taken prisoner. Most prisons were awful.

A U.S. helicopter delivers supplies to soldiers in the Vietnam War.

Word Bank

political prisoner anyone held in prison because their ideas are thought to be a threat

Caught by the enemy

Some U.S. soldiers were kept in prisons in Vietnam for a long time. Nick Rowe was one of these soldiers. For five years he was kept in a tiny prison made of sticks. It was not much more than eleven square feet (one square meter). His bed was just a straw mat. A poor diet with very few **vitamins** made him sick. His guards **tortured** him to make him tell U.S. Army secrets. They were about to kill him in the jungle when they were caught in a U.S. bombing raid. The guards ran and Rowe escaped. He was rescued and got home to the United States where he was a hero.

The cage

Prisoners in the Vietnam War were sometimes kept chained in tiny cells, unable to move. These were called "tiger cages." In the photograph below, someone is showing what they were like. The pain grew as the body began to seize up.

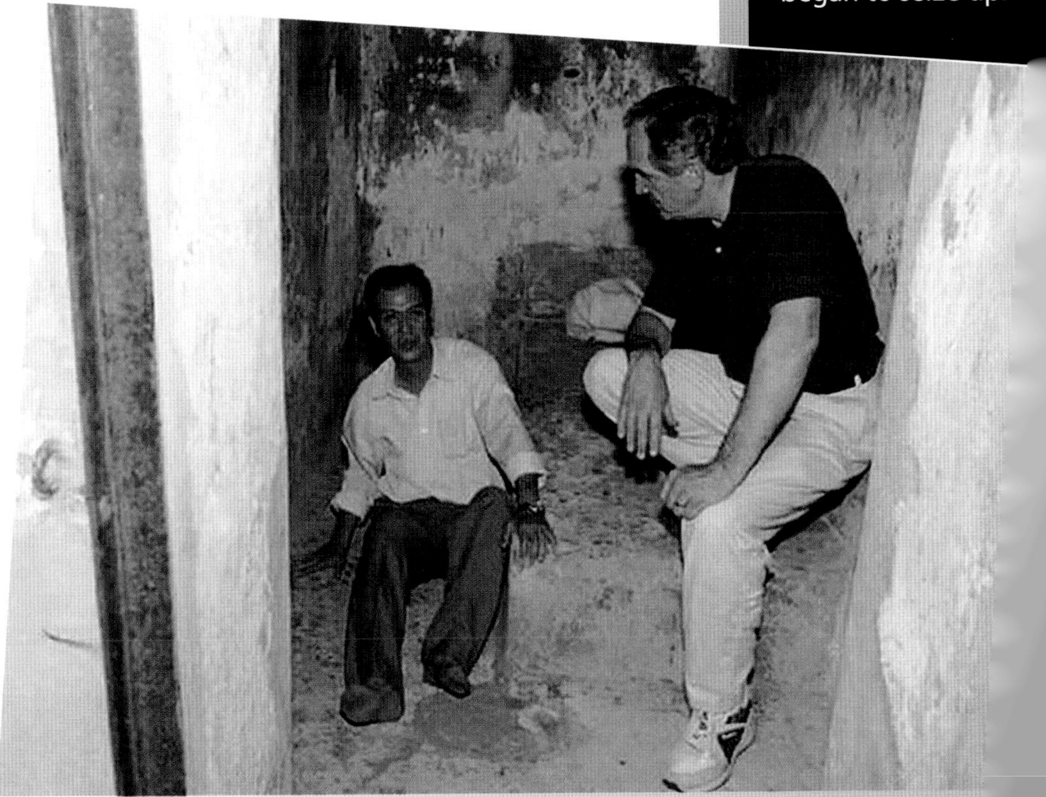

race group of people from the same region of the world and the same background

Leaving the Past Behind

Different name, same pain!

Prisons have all kinds of names. Often they are just called "jail." In the United States, a prison is often known as a **penitentiary**. Other names that prisoners give to where they have to "do time" are clink, lockup, or slammer.

Few prisons today are as terrible as those from long ago or in times of war. Some of the worst prisons of recent years have now closed. Even so, their scary names live on in stories and films.

Devil's Island

A tiny, warm island of palm trees in the Atlantic Ocean may seem like a good place to stay. But Devil's Island was far from that for almost 100 years starting in 1852. The French sent about 70,000 criminals there. Most of them never returned. Fights and murders were part of prison life there.

The prison on Devil's Island was built deep in the jungle.

Escape

Stories from Devil's Island told of sharks waiting for any prisoner who tried to swim away. Whenever a dead prisoner was "buried at sea," the chapel bell rang. That brought the sharks closer as they knew another body was on its way!

One of the prisoners on Devil's Island was Henri Charrière. He had been a safe-cracker in Paris, France, and escaped from many prisons in the 1930s. He escaped from Devil's Island by jumping off a cliff into the sea. He clung to a bag of coconuts, which he used as a raft. He succeeded in reaching the mainland. Today, the island is empty. Apart from prisoners' ghosts!

Did you know?

Prison officers still have the nickname "screws." This was after the punishment given to prisoners on a machine known as the crank. This was a small wheel turned by a handle. The punishment was to turn the handle or screw 10,000 times at over 1,000 turns per hour. Hard work—and useless!

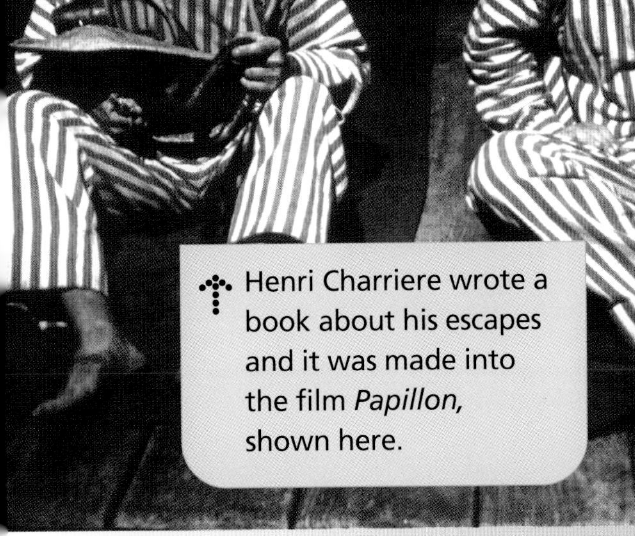

Henri Charriere wrote a book about his escapes and it was made into the film *Papillon,* shown here.

Names to chill the blood

Alcatraz Prison stood on a rocky island in San Francisco Bay. Some of the most violent prisoners were sent there from 1934 to 1963. **Gangsters** and killers ended their days there. The only way to escape was to cross the icy water with strong currents. Prisoners who tried to get away were almost always killed or caught.

Films made Alcatraz famous. Stories of its prisoners became well known. But so did the news that the prison was crumbling. The cost of keeping prisoners **secure** was too high, so it had to close. Today, Alcatraz is a museum, and more than a million tourists visit each year.

Sing Sing

New York's famous Sing Sing prison (below) was built in 1825. Since then thousands of killers have been sent there. It still locks away some of the United States' most dangerous criminals. Today Sing Sing prison has about 2,300 prisoners and 1,000 workers.

Word Bank **gangster** member of a dangerous gang of criminals

The Farm

"You're going to the Farm." Those words were enough to chill the blood of any prisoner. The Farm is the largest **maximum security** prison in the United States. It is in Angola, Louisiana. The prison started at the end of the **Civil War** in 1865. It was known for having some of the most violent prisoners in the United States.

Today the Farm has 5,000 prisoners. Most of them are serving life **sentences** for murder. They will never be let out. The prison is like a small town. It has its own radio station and newspaper. Prisoners can work to earn a small wage to spend in prison shops.

Many prisoners tried to escape Alcatraz island, but most never made it alive.

Riker's Island

Riker's Island in New York (above) is a prison island that is like a small town. It has medical clinics, baseball fields, gyms, shops, a bus station, and even a car wash. There are nine jails for men and one for women. With prisoners, staff members, and visitors, there can be up to 20,000 people on the island.

maximum security highest possible protection to stop dangerous criminals escaping

New Ways

A prisoner trains as a cook in a prison kitchen.

Prisons have come a long way. Most modern prisons are nothing like the places of pain they were in the past. They now try to do more than just punish criminals and keep them off the streets. They try to change criminals' behavior by giving help, support, and education.

In the United States and parts of Europe, many prisoners can work to earn rewards. These might be **parole** or weekend visits home. Sometimes wives or husbands are allowed in the prison to stay overnight. Prisons try to teach prisoners new skills so they can leave prison and get a job, rather than return to crime.

Did you know?

Most prisoners around the world are men. In the United States, over 90 percent of all prisoners are male. In recent years the percentage of women prisoners has more than doubled from 4 percent to 9 percent. Womens' crimes are rarely violent.

Word Bank **parole** early release of a well-behaved prisoner who is unlikely to commit more crimes

Training

Prisons will never be nice places. They will always be tough. After all, they are full of some violent people, such as murderers. That is why security has to be tight. Violence can soon break out when so many criminals are crammed together in one place. Rewards for good behavior try to make prisoners obey the rules. Punishments take away these rewards, such as having a private cell with a television, or having a choice of clothes and food.

Prisons are all about taking away people's freedom. That is the real punishment. But they should also help criminals change their behavior and learn to respect other people and the law.

For the record: Russia

Russia has about one million prisoners and 40,000 of these are women. Most of them are in the 35 women's prisons. Like men, their main crime is theft.

Prison workers try to treat prisoners fairly and help them with any problems.

Supermax

Even though prisons are far safer than they once were, they can still be dangerous places. Prisoners sometimes get killed by other **inmates.** That is why some new prisons have to be extra **secure** to cope with the most dangerous criminals. So how can such violent prisoners be controlled?

One of the answers in the United States is the new Supermax prisons. They have very strict rules and the latest **high-tech** security. Prisoners can be kept in a single cell for up to 23 hours a day. The cell is just 6 feet (2 meters) by 13 feet (4 meters). The bed is a mattress on a concrete slab.

Tough

There are over 20,000 prisoners in the United States in special Supermax security prisons or units.

"This is for the toughest of the tough. It's not a nice place. It's for doing what is necessary to protect our citizens."

(Governor Thompson, Wisconsin's Supermax.)

Supermax prisons are surrounded by huge, electric fences.

Word Bank

high-tech using the very latest technology
inmate prisoner

Extras

Some Supermax prison cells have no clocks, radios, or televisions. A camera films the prisoners all day. Computers control heavy steel doors in the prison. Workers and visitors have their hands scanned to let them through. Motion detectors and cameras record every move.

Despite all the high-tech security, some things do not change. Chains are still part of these 21st century prisons. For one hour a day, prisoners are let out of their cells to exercise. They are handcuffed and chained with at least two guards. If they still manage to break free, a deadly electric fence goes all around the prison.

Supermax
Wisconsin

Wisconsin's r
Supermax pr
was built at a
of $47.5 milli
and opened i
1999. The pris
can hold as m
as 509 inmate
in **solitary** cell
(like the one
below). There
hardly any con
with other inm
This is kept for
most dangerou
of prisoners.

solitary being totally alone

Prisons in the News

Death row

Many prisons in the United States have cellblocks kept for prisoners who are waiting to be put to death. These are known as "death row" cells. About 3,500 prisoners in the United States are on death row. Some wait a number of years before they are **executed**, usually by **lethal** injection.

Prisons will always be in the news. One of the famous prisons of recent years is at Guantánamo Bay in Cuba. This U.S. naval base was made into a prison camp to hold **terrorists.**

Since the United States declared its "war on terror," people have been held at Guantánamo Bay without **trial.** Questions have been raised about whether this should be allowed. What about the human rights of the **inmates**? Is it fair to keep people in prison without them being found **guilty** in a court of law? Boys between 13 and 15 years old have been held among about 660 inmates at Guantánamo. They were **suspected** terrorists taken to the prison from Afghanistan.

The electric chair still awaits some prisoners.

Word Bank

chain gang line of prisoners chained together and made to do heavy work

Just when you thought they had gone . . .

. . . **chain gangs** are back! In the 1990s people were surprised to see lines of prisoners out working in the United States. They were all chained together. It was just like 100 years ago!

When Alabama brought back chain gangs in 1995, it made news headlines. Then Arizona became the first state to try all-female chain gangs. Many people thought it was wrong. They said it was like going back to the cruel old days. Sheriff Joe Arpaio said, "I want everyone to see this chain gang and say, 'Prison is a very bad place to be.'"

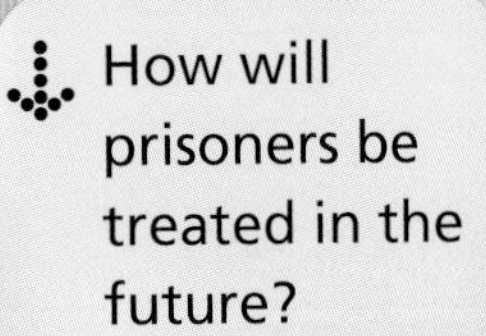

How will prisoners be treated in the future?

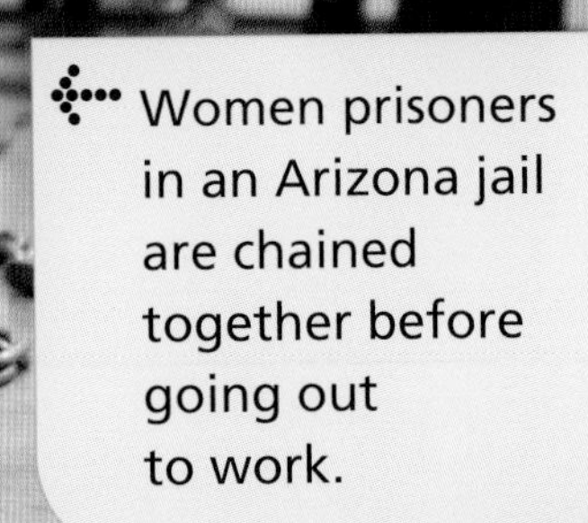

Women prisoners in an Arizona jail are chained together before going out to work.

Ending the pain

Some parts of the world still treat prisoners badly. In these places, pain and prison still go together. **Amnesty International** and other organizations try to make all prisons respect human rights. Only then will the misery that was common in so many prisons for hundreds of years be in the past for good.

lethal causing death
terrorist someone who uses fear and violence to achieve a goal

Find Out More

Did you know?

- There are about 9 million people in prisons across the world today. More than 2 million (22 percent) of them are in the United States. For many years the United States, Russia, and China have had half the world's prison population between them.

Books

Brownlie, Alison. *Crime and Punishment.* Chicago: Raintree, 2000.
Grapes, Bryan J. *Prisons.* Farmington Hills, Mich.: Greenhaven Press, 2000.
Presnall, Judith Janda. *Life on Alcatraz..* Farmington Hills, Mich.: Greenhaven Press, 2000.
Woolf, Alex. *Why Do People Commit Crime?* Chicago: Raintree, 2005.

Using the Internet

Explore the Internet to find out more about crime through time. You can use a search engine, such as www.yahooligans.com, and type in keywords such as:

- Amnesty International
- criminal
- jail.

Search tips

There are billions of pages on the Internet so it can be difficult to find exactly what you are looking for.

These search tips will help you find websites more quickly:

- Know exactly what you want to find out about first.
- Use two to six keywords in a search, putting the most important words first.
- Be precise. Only use names of people, places, or things.

1215	England	Writing of the Magna Carta (law of the land).
1253	England	Parish constables start patrolling some areas, being paid by local residents.
1475	England	**Invention** of the muzzle-loading musket.
1539	England	First criminal court established at Old Bailey.
1718	England	Machine gun invented by James Puckle.
1789	United States	U.S. Constitution **ratified.**
1829	United Kingdom	Sir Robert Peel begins a police force with 1,000 uniformed police officers, based at Scotland Yard, London.
1830	United States	First revolver made by Samuel Colt.
1833	United States	First paid police force in the United States, based in Philadelphia, Pennsylvania.
1868	United Kingdom	Last public hanging in Great Britain.
1870	United States	Creation of Department of Justice.
1878	United Kingdom	Creation of Criminal Investigation Department.
1935	United States	Bureau of Investigation becomes the Federal Bureau of Investigation (FBI).
1936	United States	Last public hanging in the United States.
1987	United Kingdom	First use of DNA typing in solving crimes.

Glossary

Amnesty International worldwide organization that campaigns for everyone to have their human rights recognized
bishop leader in the Church of England
chain gang line of prisoners chained together and made to do heavy work
civil war when soldiers from the same country fight against each other
civilized behaving with high standards and respect for others
crucified put to death by nailing the hands and feet to a cross
death sentence being sent to prison before being put to death
debtor someone who owes other people money
deducted taken away
deter put off or stop
discharge let go, or set free
dugout shelter dug in a hillside or in the ground
dungeon dark prison cell, often underground
empire area ruled by one country
execute put to death by law
fine sum of money to be paid as a punishment
first-termer prisoner who is in prison for the first time
gallows wooden structure from which prisoners were hung
gangster member of a dangerous gang of criminals
guilty having done something wrong
high sheriff officer of the government in charge of enforcing the law
high-tech using the very latest technology
illegal against the law
independent free from outside control or support
inmate prisoner
invent make or discover something for the first time
lethal causing death
maximum security highest possible protection to stop dangerous criminals escaping
merchant buyer and seller of goods to make money

oubliette dungeon with an opening only at the top, found in some old castles
parole early release of a well-behaved prisoner who is unlikely to commit more crimes
pauper very poor person who had to beg or get help from a workhouse
peasant poor person or farmworker
penitentiary type of prison
political prisoner anyone held in prison because their ideas are thought to be a threat
politician person who takes part in a political party or in government
pope leader of the Roman Catholic Church
poverty having no money or possessions
race group of people from the same region of the world and the same background
ratified to be made official
restored rebuilt and made as it once was
riot cause public violence and disorder
secure keep safe or locked up
sentence punishment set by a court of law
solitary being totally alone
suspect someone thought to have done wrong
symbol something that stands for, or represents, something else
tax charge set by leaders or government to pay for public services
terrorist someone who uses fear and violence to achieve a goal
torture causing someone great pain
trader person who buys and sells goods to make money
transportation shipping of criminals across the world to prisons or hard labor
trial hearing and judgment of a case in court
vagrant person with no job, money, or home who wanders from place to place
vitamins important chemicals in food that keep us healthy
workhouse large house where the poor stayed and worked

Index

Alcatraz Prison 36
Amnesty International 43
Australia 18, 19

Bastille 4, 22
beggars 12

cells 10, 19, 21, 23, 27, 33, 40, 41, 42
chain gangs 19, 42, 43
chains 19, 21, 41
Colditz Castle 31
crucifixion 6

death row cells 42
debtors 12, 14
deterrence 5
Devil's Island 34–35
diet 19, 30, 33
discharge fee 20
diseases 12, 17, 20, 21
dungeons 6, 8, 13, 29

Egypt 6
escapes 27, 31, 35, 36
execution 6, 42

Farm, the 37
France 4, 22
Fry, Elizabeth 25

Geneva Convention 32
Germany 30, 31
Greece 7
Guantánamo Bay 42

hard labor 15, 19
houses of correction 15
Howard, John 20
human rights 42, 43

Law of Silence 24

maximum security prisons 37, 40–41
Middle Ages 8, 10–11

Newgate Prison, London 24–25
Newgate Prison, New York 26–27

oubliettes 8–9

parole 38
paupers 14, 15
penitentiaries 23, 34
political prisoners 32
prison camps 17, 28–29
prison museums 7, 19, 29, 36
prison officers 20, 35, 39
prison reform 20–21, 23, 25, 27
prison ships 16–17
prisoners of war 16, 17, 28–31, 32, 33

reasons for prisons 5
riots 24, 25, 27
Roman prisons 6
Russia 39

"screws" 35
sentences 6, 7, 11
Sing Sing Prison 26, 36
Supermax prisons 40–41

terrorists 42
Tibet 7
"tiger cages" 33
torture 11, 22, 32, 33
Tower of London 10, 11
transportation 18–19
tread wheel 24
Turkey 9

uniforms 21, 26
United Kingdom 8, 9, 10–11, 12, 14–15, 18, 20–21, 24–25, 31
United States 13, 16, 17, 23, 26–29, 31, 34, 36–37, 40–41, 42, 43

vagrants 21
Vietnam 32–33

Walnut Street Jail 23
women prisoners 15, 17, 18, 21, 23, 25, 37, 38, 39, 43
workhouses 14, 15